VEDIC CONSCIOUSNESS

(SCIENTIFIC UNDERSTANDING)

DR. JAGADEESH PILLAI

|| MY SALUTE TO THE DIVINE SPIRIT ||

Contents

Prayer

GururBrahma GururVishnu GururDevo Maheshwaraha

Guru Saakshaat ParaBrahma Tasmai Sri Gurave Namaha

About The Author

Dr. Jagadeesh Pillai a voracious reader, Four Times Guinness World Record holder, writer, and true research scholar was born in Varanasi, the abode of Lord Shiva. He is Ph.D. in Vedic Science. He is a multi-faceted polymath with innate qualities, creative ideas and many remarkable achievements. Although his roots extend back to "Gods own Country"(Kerala), the residents of Varanasi feel proud of him and adore him as a child of Varanasi who caters to every individual in need without any expectations. A deep study into his profile reflects that he has added so many feathers to his cap which makes him quite unique. He is a four times Guinness Book of World Records Holder in the following subjects :

"Script to Screen" which he achieved by producing and directing a state of art animation film within the shortest time possible by breaking the earlier set record by Canadians. There are many national and international Awards and Recognitions to his credit.

Longest Line of Post Cards which he has done on the occasion of 163 years of Indian Postal Day by 16300 post cards. The event was also connected with a questionnaire about Indian Flag.

Largest Poster Awareness Campaign – This was achieved by designing an awareness campaign on the subject "Beti Bachao – Beti Padhao".

Largest Envelop – Towards tribute to Prime Minister's initiative 'Make in India' – he has created about 4000 sq meter envelop using waste papers.

Attempted by lighting 70000 candles on a 210 kg cake to celebrate the 70th Indian Independence day recorded in World Records India.

Attempted a documentary on Dhamek Stupa of Sarnath dubbing in 17 languages, result is waiting from Guinness World Records.

He is versatile in Gita teaching. The young generation is fond of his Gita teaching and he has changed the life of many young through his continued motivational boost up and teachings.

He has composed and sung Gayatri Mantra in 1000 different tunes.

He has composed and sung Hanuman Chalisa in 108 different tunes.

He has composed and sung hundreds of Sanskrit Bhajans, Patriotic songs, etc.

He has written and directed so many short films and documentaries for awareness campaigns.

He has done voluntary services to UP Police and Kerala Police to spread awareness campaigns on the various issue through videos and photography.

He is on the path of authoring thousands of books on Indian culture, Indian Temples, and the life of extraordinary people.

It is hard to believe that he has produced and directed more than 100 Documentaries on a particular city (Varanasi) which is done by a single person.

He has helped and guided more than 25 boys and girls to achieve world records through various creative and innovative methods.

A multifaceted person who can apply the best of his intellect using the God-given blessings which have been showered upon every human being granting them an immense capacity to learn, experience, and experiment with many things and do wonders in this world of discrimination and disparities.

He is a teacher and a student at the same time who always learns every day and teaches every day. As a master, his weakness was that he never sticks to a particular subject. Perhaps this weakness gives him the strength to master any area which he came across.

Each of his days dawned with learning a new topic and he spend most of his time experimenting and researching it.

He is also a selfless social activist and a motivational speaker.

His life was full of struggle, ups and downs, and failures. But he never gave up and faced all his trials and tribulations full of confidence. Today he is a successful young man with a lot of enthusiasm and rich life experience.

He has sung full Ram Charita Manas 51 hours audio by his own composition. He has also sung the whole Bhagavad-Gita in his own composition with a rhythmic background.

He has also sung "Lokah Samastha Sukhino Bhavantu" in 50 different languages.

Currently working on a detailed and scientific study on Veda, Upanishad, Puranas, Bhagavad Gita, etc.

Currently, he is the Hon' Chancellor of 'Eurasia Digital University'.

Awards

Four Times Guinness World Records

Winner of Mahatma Gandhi Vishwa Shanti Puraskar

Mahatma Gandhi Global Peace Ambassador
Kashi Ratna Award

Dr. APJ Abdul Kalam Motivational Person of the Year 2017

Mother Teresa Award

Indira Gandhi Priyadarshini Award

Bharat Vikas Ratna Award

Udyog Ratna Award

Vigyan Prasar Award

Poorvanchal Ratn Samman

Dr. Jagadeesh Pillai is a teacher of Vedic Science, Bhagavad Gita etc. Apart from this, he is also a Writer, Winger, Film Maker, Gemologist, Astro-Vastu Consultant, World Record Consultant, Pranic Healer, Spiritual Counsellor, Tarot Card reader etc.

He is the chairman of All India Malayali Association, Uttar Pradesh and also the National Secretary of 'Culture and Heritage' of the Indian Human Rights Association.

Preface

The Body and the Soul together we can call as Shiva and once the Soul departs its Shava (Dead Body) only. The body only activates if Soul is there. The Soul is the part of Supreme Spirit. We can say the body has Consciousness because the power of Soul exists. But most of us are unaware about the unlimited power of our consciousness.

Once the realization of the power of Soul or Consciousness happens, a person expands his way and method of living with unlimited possibilities and spread the wisdom and knowledge he has achieved to the world.

Simple explanations are given in this book to understand Vedic Consciousness.

Acknowledgements

MY INSPIRATION TO WRITE THIS BOOK

All credits humbly goes to :

My Guru

Dr. N. Gopalakrishnan Sir

Scientist (Retd) , CSIR

M.Sc. (Pharm); M.Sc. (Chem.); M.A. (Soc.); Ph.D (Bio); D.Lit

DIRECTOR

INDIAN INSTITUTE OF SCIENTIFIC HERITAGE (IISH)

National Heritage Center, Mazhuvanchery, Eranellur, Trissur 680 501

www.iish.org | E-MAIL : iishservice1@gmail.com

CHAPTER ONE

VEDIC CONSCIOUSNESS

Many people in India and Indians around the world are not deeply understanding the Indian heritage in its spiritual aspect, psychological aspect, physiological aspect, social aspect, anthropological aspect, and many other aspects including economic. So India is a country which lived on the surface of the globe earth according to archeological evidence for the last 10 thousand years. Archeological evidence based on history starts in India right from 8275 BC onwards + 2000 ad + 10 millennia. And in India, Hinduism is not a religion. We have Dharma, the way of life, the method of life. We know that on the surface of this globe earth, there are nine religions. The one Hinduism is not a religion. It's dharma which we called Sanadhana Dharma. Dharma word means; what is protecting you what is guiding you what is directing you that is dharma. Sanadhana word means never it can't be destroyed, always present here. So Sanadhana Dharma is what is violable at present in India and it is the way of life. Ayurveda is also a way of life, Yoga is a way of life, chanting a mantra, performing pooja all that is part of this way of life or method of living,

India is the only country where this dharma has got nearly 1280 fundamental literature, just like Christians have got the bible, Muslims have Kuran, and so on. But in Sanadhana Dharma the foundation literature are 1280 + 10000 commentaries in Sanskrit + more than 1 lac commentary in non-Sanskrit languages. And 1280 + 10000 + 1 lac, that is the literature treasury of India. This literature was written during last not less than 8,000 years including the oldest literature Rigveda. After that continuous addition, deletion, modification, and corrections were done. Whenever the subject becomes obsolete, deletion is to be done, wherever modifications are required, modifications are done, and wherever the thoughts become irrelevant and wrong, their correction was also done. So, addition, deletion, modification & corrections were done continuously. And everyone had the freedom to do this also. We don't need to be a super sanyasi who can only do this addition, deletion, modification and correction. In India we have never said, only my opinion is correct, in India we have never said only my religion is correct, In India we have never said only my method is correct and, in this country, we have never prevented anybody from opting for different versions. In this land, we have always allowed freedom of thought. Even from Sanadhan Dhrarma Buddhism came up, Jainism came up, Sikh religion came up. We nurtured, never prevented, never stopped never put any hindrance on that.

So, the knowledge was continuously evolving. And we integrated ancient knowledge and modern knowledge, integration of the old and the new, integration of the experienceable knowledge and experimental knowledge, and integration of spiritual knowledge and scientific knowledge, integration of physical knowledge and spiritual knowledge. As Swamy Vivekananda said what we need today is the integration of eastern knowledge and western knowledge and that is the answer to the 21st century.

And as far as we are concerned, wherever we go collect as much information as possible, convert that information into knowledge, convert the knowledge into wisdom, convert the wisdom into experience, and the totality of the experience should be our life. Repetition, collect as much information as possible, purify the information, cleans the information and convert that information into knowledge further purify the knowledge and then you will reach to the wisdom, further purify the wisdom, convert it into the experience and the total experience in our life will become our totality of the life or the life as such.

We always have to remember that preparation for living is not life. Experience of living is life. Preparation for living is not life, the experience of living is life, preparation for learning yoga is not yoga, the experience of getting yogi feeling is yoga. One may be learning yoga continuously, but that is not yoga, the experience of getting the yogic feeling that is yoga and Ayurveda is also not the preparation for learning it, the experience of adopting and adapting the ayurvedic knowledge that is real Ayurveda.

***

In fact, the west always looks from the outside, and in India, we always look from the inside. Somebody once asked; if Indian rishis could make so much knowledge but why they did not discover the gravity, Sir Issac Newton has to find out the gravity when an apple was falling on his head or nearby him. And he could easily find out the gravity from the apple.

What Indians were doing?

Indians were not looking the way in which the apple was moving. Indians were looking at how the apple seed was sprouting, the small seed was there inside, when one drop of water was falling on that or water is falling on it, it starts coming up, the plumule, the radicle, how the shell division takes place, how the cotyledons are coming, how the tree is growing, how the flowers are coming, how the co-ordination takes place, how the apple tree is coming, and how the sweetness in the apple is coming; we were looking into that - the Internal aspect of the seed. But when it is falling, external it was evaluated, but gravity was known to Indians long back

आकृष्टशिक्तश्चि मही तया यत् खस्थं गुरु स्वाभमिुखं स्वशक्त्या ।
आकृष्यते तत्पततीव भातिसमे समन्तात् क्व पतत्वयं खे ।।

Aakrushti sakthischa mahee thayaa yath
khastham svaabhimukham svasakthyaa
aakrushyathe thathpathatheeva bhaathi
same samanthaath kva pathathyayam khe

This earth attracts whatever solid materials are in the space, by her own force of attraction towards her (earth). All those subjected to this attractional force fall, to the earth. Due to equal force of attraction among the celestial bodies, where can each among them fall? (Siddhanta siromani - Bhuvanakosham 6)

1148 AD Bhaskaracharya II, Sidhanta Siromani, 6th Chapter, 21st line.

Aakrushti Sakthischa Mahee Thayaa Yath

This great earth attracts with its own force everything.

KHASTHAM

Whatever is available in the sky

SWABHIMUKHAM

Towards itself

SWASHAKTYA

By its own force

AKRISHYATE

Attracting

YAT AKRISHYATE

Whatever is getting attracted

thathpathatheeva bhaathi

Falls down

SAME SAMANTHAAT

With equal force

KVA PATATI AYAYAM KHE :

All the celestial bodies which are attracting among themselves where shall they fall, they will not fall anywhere.

That is the explanation given 500 years prior to Sir Issac Newton about gravity in a specific line for their explanation is also available in Siddhanta Shiromani.

So we were looking all the aspects. And in India, we used the Integration of science and spirituality, experienceable and experimental, the past and the future, and also every part of the knowledge we integrated.

We prayed in India

आ नो भद्राः क्रतवो यन्तु विश्वतः

(Rig Veda, I-89-1)

Let noble thoughts come towards us from all over the world.

Let it be from the Bible

Let it be from Kuran

Let it be from Communism

Let it be from Wordsworth, shelly, Tennyson or Charles dickens or from anywhere.

If good knowledge is there, let us take that without any hesitation. That is the reason why in India we had has so many literatures, so many ways of thinking, so many methods of adopting our life. Indian mind was the laboratory, the mind was the laboratory in India, and wisdom was the instrument used in India. Mind was the laboratory, wisdom was the instrument, thinking and thought process that was really the experiment done here or that was the **methodology** adopted here. And that thought process of **methodology** continued as experiments through sadhana, continuously we did sadhana, that sadhana resulted in the experiment and so much knowledge in volumes of book accumulated in India. That is the real Indian knowledge.

***

Now we will go one step more to understand Indian Knowledge.

How can we divide the Indian knowledge

Let me quote a Veda mantra

In the last chapter of Yajurveda.

ॐवद्‌यांचावद्‌यांचयस्तद्‌वेदोभयसँह।

अविद्ययामृत्युंतीर्त्वाविद्ययाऽमृतमश्नुते॥ ११॥

(11th Mantra of Isha-Upanishad.)

All Indians or non-Indians should remember at least the meaning of this line. This is the foundation of Indian knowledge :

VIDYAM CHA AVIDYAM CHA
YASTAT VEDOBHAYAM SAHA
AVIDYAYAMRITYUM TEERTHA,
VIDYAYAMRUTAMASHNUTE

There are 2 types of knowledge, one is known as Vidhya,

Vidhya and Avidhya - are the two types of knowledge available.

Vidhya is - Eternal – Experienceable - Spiritual Knowledge

Avidya is - External, Experimental - Scientific Knowledge.

AVIDYAYAMRITYUM TEERTHA

Use the scientific knowledge for overcoming the problems in our life and use the Vidhya the spiritual knowledge for attaining immortality or permanent peace.

So what have utilized the scientific knowledge for solving the day to day problems in our life and we used the spiritual knowledge for attaining immortality or permanent peace.

Do not get misunderstand that spirituality is connected with the religion. In India religion is not at all exist, its only spirituality which was and which is existing here.

One of the spiritual knowledge is yoga to attain peaceful life, mental peace and psychological peace.

So we have got 2 types of knowledge. Remember Vidhya and Avidya.

Vidhya has been divided again into two parts and Avidhya has also been divided into two parts.

Vidhya is the spiritual knowledge and in the spiritual knowledge, we have got Pure Spirituality and Applied Spirituality. In science also we got two divisions Pure Science and Applied Science.

***

Pure spirituality is the one that can only be realized through continuous sadhana. And the ultimate point of this pure spirituality we can call it as the consciousness correctly.

So the last point of spiritual knowledge is PRAGYANAM.

The word called in Vedas is "PRAGYANAM".

Prakarshena yad gyanam varthade tadeva pragyanam.

Prakarshena – gloriously

Gyanam – knowledge

Varthade – existing

That is known as pragyanam.

Every cell has got that Pragyanam. Every tissue has got that Pragyanam. Every animal has got that Pragyanam. Every living and non-living being has got that Pragyanam.

How can we say that a non-living being has got Pragyanam or that a non-living being has got consciousness?

Just take an atom.

अणोरणीयान्महतोमहीयान्
आत्मागुहायांनंहितोऽस्यजन्तोः।

Anoraneeyan mahato maheeyan, atma guhayam, nihitosya janto

(Upashidik line)

Anoraneeyan – smaller than the smallest particle

mahato maheeyan – grater than the greatest particle that is the universe itself

atma guhayam, nihitosya janto –

here we can see

in the smallest particle atom has got consciousness, the biggest particle that is the universe itself has got this consciousness and as jeevatma (soul), every living being has a soul.

Let's see, how many living being are there ?

1.6 million types of animals are there on the surface of the globe earth.

1.6 million types of animals are there on the surface of the globe earth.

4 lacs types of plants are there and 80,000 type of trees are there.

1 million type of micro-organisms are there.

In all these, whether it is micro-organisms, or a plant or a tree, or an animal ->

Intrinsic, inherent, self-guiding, self-motivating, self-energizing, awareness and consciousness are present.

And that is present in an atom.

Take the atom, in the central nucleus, is there. Electrons are revolving around it at 2182 km per second (electrons are revolving).

We have gone through approx. under graduation level that :

Electrons revolve through S orbital, B orbital, D orbital, F orbital, SP3 hybridized orbital, SP2 hybridized orbital, etc.

It's a wonder - who has created these orbitals revolving in a specific pathway.

Our highways are created by the government of India's public works department. But who has created the pathway for electrons in an atom, the nucleus is spinning 3.2 million times per second, who has given this number for that? Electrons are passing so fantastic way. Apart from that, we know that the nucleus is positively charged, and electrons are negatively charged the fundamental principle of physics tells us that positive and negative charges will be attracting each other.

The positive charge and the negative charges getting attracted but still, the electron is not falling on that. Every atom is living for about 10^{34} years and after that atom will die. In that atom all the changes are taking place without the involvement of an external agency. Without the direction from an outside source. From inside electrons know how to move, what to do,

Eg :

Sodium comes with chlorin it changes and the marriage takes place.

Sodium is poisonous material and chlorine is a poisonous gas.

These two come together we get sodium chloride (salt), which is put in the sambar.

So where that poisonous effect of that sodium has gone? Where is the poisonous effect of the chlorine gone?

They are not changed, if you are doing electrolysis, again the sodium will separate and chlorin will separate.

So non-living being (the atom) has got Intrinsic and inherent consciousness in that.

MAHATO MAHEEYAAN

The great universe has got this awareness and consciousness.

***

The famous scientist Stephen Hawkins decades ago has said there is a mother theory, M-theory, and all the other theories are coming within that as daughter theories. Mother theory is the M-theory, inside which daughter theories are coming that mother theory has constituted this universe, such billions and billions of galaxies, in each galaxy billions and billions of solar systems, in each solar systems tens and thousands of planets. Who has created it? When it was created? Who is controlling that? Who is guiding that? Some of the galaxies are expanding 8 million kilometers per second that is why in our MAHA SANKALPA some of the Poojaries chants while performing pooja, the mantra :

ADI VISHNO ADI NARAYANASYA
ACHINTIYAYA APARIMITYAYA SHAKTYAM PRIYAMANASYA
ANEKA KOTI BRAHMANDANAM MADHYE

Adi Vishnu, Maha Vishnu with limitless power in that (Aneka Kodi), billions and billions of galaxies are revolving and rotating every second and that is the universe.

No planet is colliding each other, no galaxies colliding with each other. Nothing is happening, as silent, as we can see when we are looking up either in the late evening or the night whole thing is silent and who is controlling guiding and motivating and energizing all these systems. Only one answer we can say is the “intrinsic, inherent consciousness” present in that.

And also to remember

अणोरणीयान्महतोमहीयान्
आत्मागुहायांनिहितोऽस्यजन्तोः।

As jeevatma (the soul) - we are trying through yoga to reach jeevatma, through Ayurveda We are reaching the jeevatma, through variety of Upasana we are trying to reach Jeevatma.

Indian method focuses on jeevatma and we believed that the jeevatma is presenting me and others too.

***

And remember simple statement it appears that world over we have got 757 crore people there, on the surface of the globe earth. Let us assume 800 crore or 7000 million people.

Every individual has got his nose like this down, suppose this nose is reverse and it is raining and we don't have an umbrella, what we will do. Who has decided that this nose should be down like this itself, and who has decided we should have 32 teeth? And who has decided that for males before the nose there should be moustache? And for females it need not be there.

When we are in deep sleep, the whole body system is functioning without any interruption, who is guiding that. Our heart is working at about 68, 67, and 66 times per minute. Who has decided that number, 68? and we are breathing 16 times per minute, who has fixed that number,

16 times?

We have got about 6.25-liter blood in our body, 14-gram iron is present, that 14-gram iron is continuously changing into ferrous iron and ferric iron, which is changing the biochemistry of ferrous iron and ferric iron? And why the oxygen is directly going into the ferrous iron and getting converted into ferric iron? How biochemistry can answer?

So we cannot answer all these questions. We all are taking lunch, once we put it inside, our work is over, now the work starts inside. Once a protein source reaches your stomach, hydrochloric acid and enzymes called proteases to break it down into smaller chains of amino acids. Amino acids are joined together by peptides, which are broken by proteases. From our stomach, these smaller chains of amino acids move into our small intestine. All the carbohydrates are to be digested by the amylases. And vitamin E, vitamin A, vitamin B, C, D, E, and K should never get destroyed. It should be taken from the food and should be transferred through the blood and it should reach - A should reach the eyes, K should reach to the skin, C should reach our cycle Kreb cycle or Citric acidic cycle. Who is taking all these?

We are and always say that we are great. But in fact, our greatness is nothing.

Whole-body system is functioning in such a fantastic way without external involvement.

Just look ourselves, that is why in ancient time the scholars used to say:

Realization of the self is the final answer.

Let's look into our eyes, how the eyes are looking at others, the image is falling in the retina, vitamin A present in that, getting converted into retinoic acid, the electricity generated is taken to the video nervous system (video – nervous system to the correct center) there it is getting analyzed and we will say that in front of us Mr. So and so and Mrs. so and so is standing.

How fantastic our brain is analyzing, if we give a speech or talk to somebody continuously without interruption how the words are coming to our brain and that message going to our vocal cord. The vocal cord vibrates, all the muscles are supporting that, the correct English words are coming, those English words are passing through the mic (if the mic is there), and we will listen through the amplifier because it touches the ear. And our eardrum is vibrating, for that 55-micron electricity is produced there – thus we are able to understand the conversation or speech.

***

BODY MECHANISM

What is the mechanism going on in this great body?

Remember, this is the consciousness present in our body.

No further answer is required.

YAT CHAKSHUSHA NA PASHYATI

YE NA CHAKSHUM SHI PASHYATI

This consciousness we cannot see through your eyes.

YAT CHAKSHUSHA NA PASHYATI

We cannot see it., but

YE NA CHAKSHUM SHI PASHYATI

What makes the eye see the other thing that is consciousness.

When we are sitting and looking at somebody, for 14 minutes our right eyes are working and after that our right eyes will take a rest and left eye will be working and after 14 minutes again right eye will be working. This change is taking place, who is changing this? We cannot answer. So

आत्मागुहायांनहितोऽस्यजन्तोः।

every living being, every cow knows which grass it can eat. Every monkey knows which fruits it can eat. Every crow knows which foods it can eat. Every animal on the surface of the globe earth knows pretty well what are the food meant for that. How this intrinsic, inherent knowledge exists. It is given to them by birth. That is what we say

YAT STOTHRENA NASHRUNOTI

Even if I try to explain it to anybody, through the ears understanding is difficult.

But **YENA STOTRAMITAM SUTAM**

What makes your ears understand that that biochemical process is controlled and guided by the consciousness.

In Vedas, it is told,
YATO VACHO NIVARTHANTE APRAPYA MANASA SAHA

A yoga teacher should start teaching yoga by telling this line.

Yato vaacho nivartande - the words are coming back from that point

aprapya manasa saha - The mind also returning from that point, because the mind cannot reach that level

The words cannot reach that level, without reaching the last point the whole thing comes back from the ultimate, that is the absolute consciousness.

That's why the beautiful definition is there

NA TATHRA SOORYO BHAATI - that absolute consciousness you are taking.

There the light of the sun has got nothing to do.

Na tatra sooryo bhaati, Na Chandra tarakam

No moon no stars has got any influence upon this one.

Nema vidhyuto bhanti - the lightning, fantastic light in the electric energy produced in the lightning.

One engineer was explaining how much electricity is there in the fantastic super lightening.

He said: How much electricity is needed for New York City for 8 years, that much electricity is there in one lightening.

So that lightning has cannot come nearer to this consciousness which is present in every living.

So

Na tatra sooryo bhaati, Na Chandra tarakam
Nema vidhyuto bhanti
Kutoyamagnihi, tameva bhantam anubhati sarvam
Tasya basa vishwamitam vibhatim

That gives them energy to everything, that lights everything, that guides everything, that motivates everything. That is instructing everything.

And the topmost man President of America and also the ordinary man who runs a tea shop that particular consciousness is guiding.

***

PURE SPIRITUALITY

"PRAGYANAM BRAHMA".

And we Indians call - "PRAGYANAM BRAHMA".

"Pragyanam Brahma" is that glorious inherent, intrinsic, awareness, and consciousness present in all living and non-living beings.

That was the principle here.

That is basic spirituality.

And reaching up to that much is very difficult.

Because very clearly

NA TATHRA CHAKSHUR GACHATI

It's very difficult to explain to anyone.

Na tatra chakshur gachati – I cannot really see it.

Na vag gachati - the words will not reach there.

Na manaha – the mind will not reach there.

Na vitmo - no body knows about it.

The rishi's said nobody knows about it.

na vijanimo – there is nobody who can teach about it.

Anusheshyaat. – how can I teach anybody these things.

And he said, I cannot teach you these things.

Because words will not reach there, our mind will not reach there and our eyes will not reach there.

That is what we can re-imagine if possible, if we have reached that level, then go all imagining through sadhana. Make the mind as the laboratory. Our wisdom, the instrument, and also our thoughts, thinking power, should be really literally the thinking power is to be the **methodology for research** and all the sadhana is the experiment and then we will get the knowledge. And that knowledge when we are getting we will realize that everywhere this consciousness is present. We are also the abode of that consciousness.

And once we have reached that level.

NA TANTHRAM, NA DHYANAM NA SHAYANAM NA YAGYO PAVEETAM

Nothing is required.

Na mantram – mantram is not required

Na dhyanam – dhyanam is not required

Na shayanam – sleeping is not required

Na shaucham – cleansing the body is not required

Because we have crossed that level.

***

Once Alexander the Great came to India.

He promised his mother when he was making a round of his own travel and when he was back home, his mother said you are a great warrior, I would like to request you one thing, before my death, I would like to drink a little bit of Ganga water. Can you bring that Ganga water to me?

Then The Alexander promised his mother, I will bring the whole country to you, don't worry about Ganga alone.

I will bring the whole country. Then his mother said, that is the country known as Bharatam. Bharatam means mix of BHAVAM, RAGAM, THALAM. It's a musical country.

That country, therefore the last 8000 years, the country has never invaded any other country. But anyone who invaded that country those fellows have never come back.

And this is what Alexander's mother told to Alexander.

Then also Alexander said, still I will bring Ganga water, and he was specifically informed by his mother that that is the country where people could really realize the divine power. They have seen the god directly. Then later Alexander came here and enquired to many people if anybody has seen God? Can anyone can show one person who has seen God?. He asked many people. Finally, there was one rishi, Piplada Muni. Alexander came directly to Piplada Muni, promised that I will give everything to you, can you show me the god. Muni kept quiet. Then he said. I will give you half of the countries which I have conquered on the way from Greek to this place.

Then Muni said, who wants the looted material. Who wants the conquered country and other things. Do you think that it will be remaining like that when you go back?

Again and again the question came, finally,

Alexander said, I shall give you everything, including my crown and the ornament and all whatever you want – just show me the God.

Then towards Alexander Piplada Muni said,

I need only one thing, Alexander became happy because this fellow wants something.

So, then Piplada Muni said, till now the sunrise used to fall me directly but your horse is there in between now. You remove that horse.

That is the only thing, that I want.

So

Na mantram, na tantram, na dhyanam

Na shayanam , Na shaucham, na yagyopavitam,

Na dandam, na shika, na kamdalu

Nothing is required because you have crossed that limit, there stands consciousness.

Swimming cannot be learned by postal tuition, and can't be learned by reading a book – it can only be learned by jumping into water.

Yoga is like that and Ayurveda is also like that.

All the 642 chemicals which are used in modern medicine has got side effects and deleterious poisonous effects are there. Whereas Ayurveda if properly used does not have that. Ayurvedic medicines do not have side effects because it is integrating spirituality and science. It is integrating old knowledge and modern knowledge, it is integrating experienceable knowledge and experimental knowledge. These are explained in the slokha :

SAKSHAAT ANUBHAVAYADRISHTO

NA SHRUTO, NA GURU DARSHITA,

LOKANAM UPAKARAYA,

YEDAT SARVAM PRADRSHITAM

Sakshaat, anubhavayadrishto – they have understood all

these things from their experience.

Sakshat – directly

Anubhavayadrishto – experienced

Na shruto - not learned or heard from anywhere.

Na guru darshita – don't think that these are all given by the Guru.

They have given experiments from within themselves.

And then they have reached here.

Na shruto Na guru darshita - all these messages are given to the world, **LOKANAM UPAKARAYA**

For the benefit of the people, not for making money, not for becoming rich - but for the benefit of the people.

LOKANAM UPAKARAYA
EDAT SARVAM PRADARSHITAM

That is the reason J.C.Bose did not patent the wireless. J.C.Bose did not patent any of his knowledge, any of his tools, any of his instruments. He said 3000 years before my forefathers sat on the banks of Ganga and whatever knowledge they have developed, they have never patented it and I am a follower of them and I do not want to patent that. So J.C. Bose's knowledge was there at Cambridge University, Marconi was sitting behind that and after 11 months Marconi patented it in his name. At that time, the patenting officer said, you are doing plagiarism, and was not allowed. Finally, Marconi came to J.C. Bose and requested his permission for his patenting.

So Marconi got the patent.

1998 Scandinavian University decided that the inventor or the discoverer, whether he likes or not if the public knows that it belongs to that person patent should go to that person.

In 1998 onwards it has been proved that wireless has been discovered by J.C. Bose.

All general knowledge book published the world over except in India, contains this message.

So Indian knowledge has been given to everyone.

So this is the Indian spirituality going to the last point.

Every question can be answered by this method.

Why we are closing our eyes, because the intrinsic, inherent, awareness is there in the eyelid, that is why we are closing the eyes. One hour left nose is working and after one-hour right nostril is working. How and why this change is happening?

Awareness and consciousness are present in this one, that is why it is working.

Why we are becoming anime because it is not in a position to collect iron present in the food because of phytanic acid disease. So the body is showing you the inability to collect the iron from the food system. Why, the awareness, and consciousness are functioning in such a way that it is demonstrated outside that you are anime. So, we are forced to take more iron. So, this is the principle of Ayurveda. So Ayurveda tells you :

YOGAATAVI VISHAM TEEKSHNAM
BHAVET BHAISHAJYAMUTTAMAM
BHAISHAJYAMATIDURYUKTAM
BHAVET TEEKSHNAM VISHAM

Anything can be utilized as a medicine, provided your body can accommodate that. Even poison can be utilized as a medicine, provided your body needs that.

Yogaatavi - by proper combination

Teekshnam visham – deadly poisonous materials can be used as a medicine if the proper combination is done. But even though a perfect medicine if not properly given that will become poison for our body.

So, what is connected directly with the body is consciousness.

And also see

SAREERA MANASO YOGA, PARASPARA MANURVAJE
AADHAARA ADHEYA BHAVENA

TAPTAGYA GATAYORIVA

All the principle put forward by Dr. Deepak Chopra, are based on this line.

In Dr. Deepak Chopra's theory, all new age therapy is based on this Sanskrit line from Charaka Samhita.

SAREERA MANASO YOGA

Mind and body are complementary to each other.

ADHAARA ADHEYA BHAVENA

Body is the support mind is the one which is getting the support.

TAPTA-GYA KHATAYORIVA

This comparison is very important

It is called

Tapta – Agya – khata – yo - riva

Taptam – heat

Agyam – ghee

Khatam – vessel

iva - light that

like the ghee and the vessel relation. What is the relation between the vessel and the ghee?

Hot ghee is poured into a cold vessel, heat will transfer from the ghee to the vessel. When the cold ghee is poured into the hot vessel, heat will transfer from the vessel to the ghee. Just like that, the positives and the negatives of the mind will be having a direct bearing on the body

The positive and negatives of the body will be having a direct bearing upon the mind.

So first treat the mind before treating the body like in Yoga.

What would be the exact definition of yoga :

It can be explained from Rigveda

TRI-SAPTA SAMITAKRITAAHA

DEVA-YAD-YAGYAM

TANWANAA-ABADHNAN PURUSHAM PASHUM

YAGYENA YAGYAMAYAJANTA

DEVASTHAANI DHARMAANI

PRATHAMAYAASAN

Tre-sapta-samitakritaaaha

Three...in English and Sanskrit, it is Three only.

Three means, three

Sapta means, septa – 7

Three sapta - 3x7

Samitakritaha – putting together

3x7 putting together

3x7 is 21

what is this 21 putting together

i.e.

Pancha-jyanendriya

Pancha-karmendriya

Pancha-bhootah

Pancha prana + mind

Just calculate how much is there.

Pancha prana – 5

Pancha jyanendriya – 5

Pancha karmendriya – 5

Pancha prana – 5

Plus – one – mind - 21

Samitakritaha – put together

And all the animal instincts present in that just discard from that and replace “purusham pashum apagnan” – put dharmic values in that.

This must be the beginning part of yoga.

Yoga means – bringing together.

Yuj is the root of the word.

Yoga bringing together.

Bringing together of pancha prana, pancha bhoota, pancha jyanendriya and pancha karmendriya + mind together is yoga.

And in that yoga we can see that the mind is working there, Prana is working there, Gyanendra is working there, Karmendriya is working there –the whole human body is working there.

When the prana flows - the ears are working, the eyes are working, the tongue is working, the heart is working and the skin is working. Every bit of the body is functioning even though we are sleeping or jagrat, swapna, sushupti awasta, whole system is working without our involvement in that, we are the only carrier of our own system. We do not know what are the things happening inside our bodies luckily, if we know what are the things happening inside our bodies, we will be unconscious.

If a fat lady, or fat man, is subjected to surgery and if we are looking inside his body, we are out, we will be falling down. So, since beautiful skin is there outside, we look and say that that man is very handsome and beautiful excellent good morning, sir, but if we are looking inside, absolutely such an ugly thing right from the 22 ft. intestine itself carries all the dirt just like the, our external channel which is carrying the dirt. From A to Z, drainage channel, you know 22ft long intestine is carrying all the chapatti and all the food we eat. It is also passing through that one, even though it is tasty, the taste is only there for the 9 cm tongue. After that the taste is not there, nothing is there. This 9 cm tongue create all the problem for us.

And that is why we say, we are facing three problems, hurry, worry & curry.

And this is because of this tongue.

And so knowing that absolute where it is impossible to explain that is the spirituality there.

APPLIED SPIRITUALITY

Already mentioned earlier about +Pure Spirituality and

Applied Spirituality.

That applied spirituality, that mantra we used to chat closing your eyes, folding your hands

SAHANA VAVATU, SAHANOU BHNAKTU

SAHAVEERYAM KARA VA VAHAI

TEJASVINAVADHEETAMASTU

MA VID VISHA VAHAI

Why we chant this mantra, because the **PRAGYANAM,** consciousness is present in me. So **AHAM BRAHMASMI**

That consciousness is present in others

TATWA MASI

That consciousness is present in all living being,

AYAMATMA BRAHMA

These are the beauty of Maha Vakyas

One - Pragyanam Bahma – from Rigveda

Second - Aham Brahmasmi - Yajurveda

Third -Tatwamasi – Samaveda

Fourth - Ayamatma Brahma – Adharva Veda

Four Vedas gives four Maha vakya – great messages.

Maha means – great

Vakya means – messages

so

Aham brahmasmi – I am the embodiment of the god.

You are also the embodiment of the god.

So we too are the manifestation and manipulation of divine power.

So what is our relation?

Our relation is - We are the manifestation of the same power.

So we are brothers and sisters, we are the family members

VISHWAM BHAVATI EKA NEEDAM

The whole world is like one nest, and different types of birds are coming there.

They make different noises and voices, and they sing beautifully, but this world is just like a nest where all birds are coming

VISHWAM BHAVATI EKA NEEDAM

The reason is that

I am the manifestation of the divine power.

You are also the manifestation of the divine power

That is why Indians do NAMASTE

THEY – NAMAHA

I am doing namaskaram to you because you are the embodiment of the divine power, I am also the embodiment of the divine power. So we have to exist together here.

SAHANA VAVATU, SAHANOU BHNAKTU

(we have to share the result of the work together)

SAHAVEERYAM KARA VA VAHAI

(we have to work together)

TEJASVINAVADHEETAMASTU

(we have to enlighten ourselves together)

MA VID VISHA VAHAI

(Never we should have hatred towards anybody else) no hatred against,

आनोभद्राः क्रतवोयन्तुविश्वतः

(let noble thought come towards us from all over the world)

your thought shares it, my thought shares it.

Let us take good from everywhere.

भद्र ंकर्णभिः शृणुयाम देवा

(this is applied spirituality)

let us listen to this glorius message)

भद्र ंपश्यमेाक्षभिर्यजत्राः

(let us see glorious sceneries in front of us)

स्थरिरैङ्गैस्तुष्टुवांसस्तनूभिर्व्यशेम देवहितं यदायुः

(as long as we are living here on the surface of the globe earth let us do the best thing possible in our life.

CALCULATION OF LIFE

Let's calculate how many days one will be living – it's very simple, even a calculator is not required.

Let's assume our approx. Healthy life 75 year x 365, the number of hours x 60, the to know the number of minutes x 60 once again, to know the number of second x 60 once again.

So that is 26500 days we are living here.

26500 days you are living here on the surface of the globe earth.

Every day we are breathing 23080 times.

And according to T. S. Eliot, a fantastic poet, every breath is taking us towards graveyard.

So we all are moving, that trip, that traveling started right from the date of birth, it will be ending on the date of death.

DOB & DOD – remember these very important abbreviations.

DOB & DOD – in between these two - revolutionary changes will take place internally and evolutionary change will take place externally

Internally – revolutionary change should take place.

Externally – evolutionary change should take place.......

Internally violent change should take place, and externally silent change should take place.

This is what we needed between DOB & DOD.

According to the Indian system, if one fellow is living for about 70 years, he takes 60 tons of food and generally, it becomes a waste. Whatever may be our designation, whether we have got PHD or D.Litt. or anything else, once we have died and our body is put on the firewood, and the fire is given, 58-gram ash.

Nothing else

that is calcium oxide, potassium oxide, sodium oxide, zinc

oxide, little bit iron oxide, and silicon oxide that's all, 9 more micro constituents will be there.

So remember that we think we are something great, we have to be proud of ourselves, as every English line you can see - when we write they-we-he-she and so on in between a line all small letter but whenever we write "I", I is capital letter because I am proud of my myself.

This is ok. But don't get elevated from that level. Beyond that we are nothing.

Last century this day we were not here, next century this day we will not be here.

So after all why we are here.

Simply we are coming here, sitting here, destroying some food, and going back.

So our applied spirituality passes through the philosophy also.

These are the philosophical information.

So spirituality and applied spirituality are like Pure Science and Applied Science.

When our consciousness work we can get a lot of knowledge by sadhana.

The Delhi Iron Piller, is not rusting, absolutely no rusting. It is remaining intact, technologically iron it could handle very nicely.

Ajanta cave temple, Ellora cave temple, the marvelous civil engineering that we can see. Variety of temples in Tamil Nadu and Kerala. How could they make it? The Portland cement was produced in 1920 in England. The first ship of Portland cement came from England to India in 1922, but our buildings are here for the last 800 years, 900 years, and thousand of years. Absolutely no problem. No guarantee nobody has given, but still that painting is there. So technologically we were not,

Our Kanchipuram saree, which was exported to Rom in BC-600 was from Banaras, and the whole pyramid was carved by the chisel taken from Banaras. Our Technology means Indian technology was also not bad.

What we have to convey to all people is pure spirituality, applied spirituality, pure science, and applied science.

In these 4 branches, we can see continuously addition, deletion, modification, and correction are done. Integrated spirituality and science, integrated old and modern knowledge, integrated experienceable and experimental knowledge, 8000+2000, 10000 years history of India. It is the history of the world because we consider everyone as one.

This earth itself is our mother, all the children of this earth. So wherever we are belonging whether we belong to America or Brazil or South America or Europe or Africa, we are all the embodiment and the manifestation of the same divine power. So, that relation is the best relation.

Freedom for everything.

Freedom for becoming an atheist also.

Freedom for chanting a mantra, not chanting a mantra.

Nobody will be protesting and nobody will be worried about it.

Because it is a smooth democratic system existed here for the last 10 millennia.

That is the reason why out of the 49 civilizations existed on the surface of the globe earth, 48 civilizations got vanished here, with only one remaining. That is this country India which is still existing.

We never prayed that only our people should reach heaven.

Only our religion should spread.

Only our book should be read.

We prayed SARVE BHAVANTU SUKHINAHA
(let everyone become happy, healthy and enjoy the life)

Nobody should feel the pain of that one.

We Prayed

LOKAHA SAMSTHAHA SUKHI NO BHAVANTU

We never payed

HINDUTWA SAMSTHA SUKHINO BHAVANTU

www.ingramcontent.com/pod-product-compliance
Ingram Content Group UK Ltd.
Pitfield, Milton Keynes, MK11 3LW, UK
UKHW042000190726
13854UKWH00005B/2090